AUSTRALIA
the land

Erinn Banting

A Bobbie Kalman Book

The Lands, Peoples, and Cultures Series

Crabtree Publishing Company

www.crabtreebooks.com

The Lands, Peoples, and Cultures Series

Created by Bobbie Kalman

Coordinating editor
Ellen Rodger

Project editor
Carrie Gleason

Production coordinator
Rosie Gowsell

Project development, photo research, design, and editing
First Folio Resource Group, Inc.
  Erinn Banting
  Tom Dart
  Söğüt Y. Güleç
  Claire Milne
  Jaimie Nathan
  Debbie Smith

Prepress and printing
Worzalla Publishing Company

Consultants
Jamie Breadmore; Amanda Burdon; Frank Povah, The Busy
Boordy

Photographs
Kathie Atkinson/AUSCAPE: p. 27 (top); Bill Bachman: title
page, p. 3, p. 11 (top), p. 18 (bottom), p. 19 (bottom), p. 20 (left),
p. 21 (bottom), p. 23 (left), p. 24 (right); Bill Bachman/Photo
Researchers: p. 21 (top); Corbis/Magma Photo News, Inc./
Bettmann: p. 13 (bottom); Corbis/Magma Photo News, Inc./
Dave G. Houser: cover; Corbis/Magma Photo News, Inc./
Christine Osborne: p. 12 (right); Corbis/Magma Photo News,
Inc./Reuters NewMedia Inc.: p. 15 (top left); Corbis/Magma
Photo News, Inc./Stuart Westmorland: p. 31 (top, bottom
right); Marc Crabtree: p. 4, p. 5 (bottom), p. 7 (left), p. 22
(bottom), p. 26 (right); Chad Ehlers/International Stock:
pp. 16–17; Jean-Paul Ferrero/AUSCAPE: p. 5 (top), p. 15
(bottom), p. 20 (right), p. 25 (bottom), p. 27 (bottom),
p. 28 (right), p. 29 (top right); Jim Frazier/AUSCAPE: p. 23
(right); Rob Gilley/ImageState: p. 6; François Gohier/
AUSCAPE: p. 31 (bottom left); Joseph Green/Life File: p. 12
(left); Rob Griffith/Associated Press, AP: p. 13 (top); Dennis
Harding/AUSCAPE: p. 25 (top left); C. Andrew Henley/
AUSCAPE: p. 24 (left); Miwako Ikeda/International Stock:
p. 18 (top); Guy Lamothe/AUSCAPE: p. 22 (top); Jean-Marc
La Roque/AUSCAPE: p. 25 (top right); Victor Last: p. 19 (top);
Wayne Lawler/AUSCAPE: p. 9 (bottom); Tom McHugh/Photo
Researchers: p. 27 (middle); Reg Morrison/AUSCAPE: p. 9
(top); Mark Newman/International Stock: p. 10 (top); Richard
T. Nowitz: p. 15 (top right); D. Parer & E. Parer-Cook/
AUSCAPE: p. 7 (right); Michael Peck/ImageState: p. 26 (left);
Pieternella Pieterse/Panos Pictures: p. 14; Jeff Rotman/Photo
Researchers: p. 29 (left); Becca Saunders/AUSCAPE: p. 30
(top); John Shaw/AUSCAPE: p. 28 (left); Paul Thompson/
International Stock: p. 17 (top); Neil Vincent/AUSCAPE: p. 30
(bottom); David Wachenfeld/AUSCAPE: p. 29 (middle right);
S. Wilby and C. Ciantar /AUSCAPE: pp. 10–11

Map
Jim Chernishenko

Illustrations
Dianne Eastman: icon
David Wysotski, Allure Illustrations: back cover
MikeCarterStudio.com: p. 4, p. 8

Cover: Massive, crescent-shaped sand dunes, known as "the
Walls of China," stand in Mungo National Park, in New South
Wales. The dunes cover more than 18 miles (30 kilometers).

Title page: Fishing boats crowd the Victoria Dock, in Hobart,
Tasmania. Fishers in Tasmania catch mainly rock lobsters and
abalones, which are types of shellfish.

Icon: Koala bears, which appear at the head of each section,
spend most of their time in eucalyptus trees, munching on
leaves or sleeping. Koalas spend an average of 21 hours
sleeping or resting each day.

Back cover: When baby kangaroos, or joeys, are born, they are
the size of a bean. Joeys spend 33 weeks inside their mother's
pouch, by which time they are too large to be carried around.

Published by
Crabtree Publishing Company

PMB 16A,	612 Welland Avenue	73 Lime Walk
350 Fifth Avenue	St. Catharines	Headington
Suite 3308	Ontario, Canada	Oxford OX3 7AD
New York	L2M 5V6	United Kingdom
N.Y. 10118		

Cataloging in Publication Data
Banting, Erinn.
  Australia. The land / Erinn Banting.
    p. cm. -- (Lands, peoples, and cultures series)
Includes index.
Summary: Text and photographs portray Australia's unique
geography, wildlife, and climate, as well as its city and rural
life, industry, and transportation.
  ISBN 0-7787-9343-5 (RLB) -- ISBN 0-7787-9711-2 (pbk)
  1. Australia--Description and travel--Juvenile literature. [1.
Australia.] I. Title. II. Series.
  DU105.2 .B46 2003
  994--dc21
                                          2002013727
                                          LC

Contents

4 An island continent

6 The Land Down Under

10 Welcome to the outback!

12 Wild weather

14 The Australians

16 Coastal cities

20 Crops, livestock, and fishing

22 Changing industries

24 What grows in Australia?

26 Amazing animals

29 Danger in the wild

30 Life on the Great Barrier Reef

32 Glossary and Index

An island continent

Earth did not always look as it does today. Hundreds of millions of years ago, it was covered by one enormous landmass called Pangaea. About 200 million years ago, Pangaea began to split in two. Slowly, the two pieces drifted farther apart and split into even more pieces. Eventually, the seven continents formed: North America, South America, Europe, Asia, Africa, Australia, and Antarctica. Australia and Antarctica drifted the farthest south, into the **southern hemisphere**.

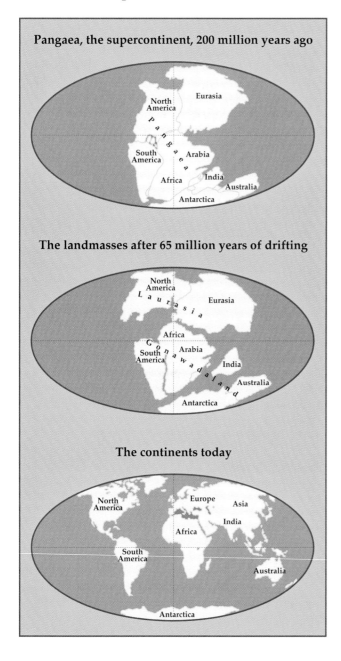

Pangaea, the supercontinent, 200 million years ago

The landmasses after 65 million years of drifting

The continents today

Australis

About 1,800 years ago, Ptolemy, an ancient Greek geographer, included Australia on one of the earliest maps of the world. He named the island continent *Terra Australis Incognita*, which means "unknown southern land." Australia gets its name from the **Latin** word *Australis*, which means "southern." The smallest of the seven continents, Australia is the only continent to hold just one country. It is divided into six states: Queensland, New South Wales, Victoria, South Australia, Western Australia, and Tasmania. It also has two territories on the mainland — the Northern Territory and the Australian Capital Territory — and eight territories that are islands, including Christmas Island and Norfolk Island. Australia also claims ownership of nearly one-third of Antarctica.

Gray kangaroos are one of Australia's national symbols.

Nowhere else in the world

Australia's geography and wildlife are unlike anywhere else in the world. Sunny beaches, lush farmland, and busy ports line the coasts. In the center of the country is a vast area known as the outback, with hot, treacherous deserts, unusual rock formations, and sheep and cattle ranches, or stations, that are as large as some European countries. Off Australia's northeast coast lies the world's largest coral reef, the Great Barrier Reef. Throughout all these landscapes, animals such as kangaroos, koalas, kookaburras, and crocodiles hop, climb, fly, and swim.

Brisbane's office towers, shopping malls, and houses crowd a section of the east coast called the Gold Coast.

Facts at a glance
Official name: Commonwealth of Australia
Area: 2,940,521 square miles (7,617,930 square kilometers)
Population: 19,357,594
Capital: Canberra
Official language: English
Main religions: Protestant, Roman Catholic
National holiday: January 26 (Australia Day)

The land around the Mount Alma Range, part of the South Australian outback, is dry and pebbly, with few shrubs.

The Land Down Under

Australia is so far away from North America that people traveling from the United States or Canada lose a day on their way there and gain a day on their way home. Australia is often called "the Land Down Under" because of its distance from many places and because it is entirely in the southern hemisphere.

A long coastline

Along Australia's 22,826 miles (36,727 kilometers) of coastline are long stretches of beaches, rocky cliffs, **fertile** farmland, and bustling cities, especially in the east and south. Some sections of the coast have special names. The Gold Coast, which stretches from the eastern city of Brisbane south to the New South Wales border, is named for its beaches of white sand that look golden in the sunshine. The Sunshine Coast refers to the sun-filled beaches north of Brisbane up to the town of Gympie. Swimming along the coasts can be dangerous because of rips, or rip currents. These powerful currents can sweep anything in their path, including people, out to the ocean.

(top) Massive rock pillars known as the Twelve Apostles stand off the south coast of Victoria. The pillars were once part of the mainland, before being worn away by the wind and water.

Ancient mountains

The mountains along Australia's coasts are made from some of the oldest rocks known to humans. The Great Dividing Range runs parallel to the east coast, from Queensland to Victoria. Steep, narrow gorges separate this series of mountains, which include Mount Kosciuszko, in the southeast. At 7,309 feet (2,228 meters), Mount Kosciuszko is the mainland's highest peak.

A curious phenomenon takes place in the Blue Mountains, which are part of the Great Dividing Range, near Sydney. Eucalyptus trees in the mountain's forests release oil into the air. When the sun passes through the oil drops, the mountains seem to turn blue. The Blue Mountains are also home to sandstone pillars known as the Three Sisters. According to a legend told by the Katoomba, an **Aboriginal** people, the pillars were once three sisters who fell in love with three brothers from another Aboriginal group. Their union was forbidden. The brothers did not accept this and tried to capture the sisters. They did not succeed because a **clever-man** used his special powers to protect the sisters, turning them into stone.

(right) Lake Eyre only fills with water once or twice every 100 years. When the lake is dry, it is covered with a crusty sheet of salt.

(below) The clever-man who changed the three sisters into sandstone pillars was killed in a battle between the two groups before he could change the pillars back into girls.

Playas

In the desert, flat basins called playas fill with water when it rains, and then quickly dry up again. The water seeps into the ground or **evaporates** into the air, leaving behind salt or clay. In parts of Australia where rain is rare, especially in the south and west, playas, which are also called salt pans or clay pans, can be completely dry for years. Lake Eyre is the largest playa in Australia.

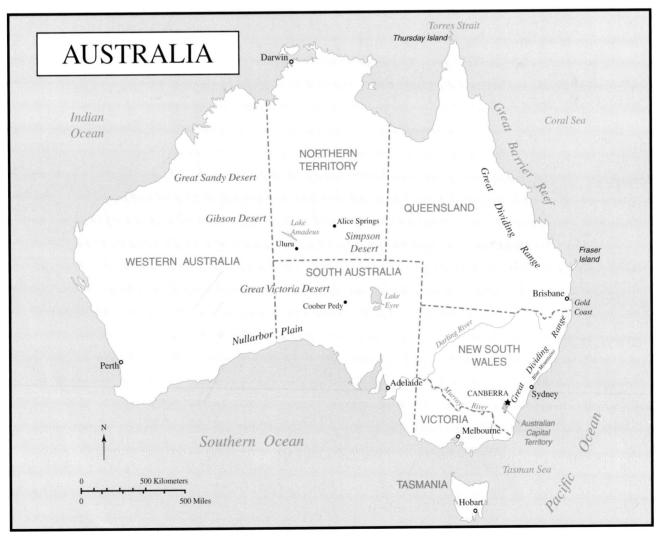

AUSTRALIA

Torres Strait
Thursday Island
Darwin

Indian Ocean

Coral Sea

NORTHERN TERRITORY

Great Sandy Desert

Great Dividing Range

Great Barrier Reef

QUEENSLAND

Gibson Desert

Lake Amadeus
Alice Springs

Simpson Desert

Fraser Island

Uluru

WESTERN AUSTRALIA

SOUTH AUSTRALIA

Great Victoria Desert

Lake Eyre

Brisbane
Gold Coast

Coober Pedy

Darling River

Nullarbor Plain

NEW SOUTH WALES

Great Dividing Range

Blue Mountains

Perth

Adelaide

Murray River

CANBERRA
Sydney

VICTORIA

Australian Capital Territory

N

Melbourne

Southern Ocean

Tasman Sea

Pacific Ocean

0   500 Kilometers
0   500 Miles

TASMANIA

Hobart

Billabongs

When rivers in Australia dry up, they leave behind small ponds of water called billabongs. Billabongs also form when slow-moving rivers change course, and parts of the river get cut off. The water in these sections has nowhere to go, so it becomes **stagnant**. These areas of still water are surrounded by plant life and attract many animals, including crocodiles, pelicans, and cockatoos. In areas where rivers flow throughout the year, such as in the Murray-Darling Basin, in the southeast, the land is more fertile and farmers grow crops. Forty-two percent of Australia's farmland is fed by the Murray and Darling Rivers.

Tropical forests

In northern Australia, monsoon, or dry tropical, forests are home to plants, trees, and animals that have **adapted** to long dry periods during the winter and heavy rainfall in the summer. In these forests, some types of eucalyptus trees survive by storing water in their roots during dry periods. In the fertile, mild **rainforests** of the Great Dividing Range, milkwood, palm, ironwood, and wattle trees grow. Australia does not have as many rainforests as it once did, especially in the east where many were cut down for firewood and to make room for farms and cities.

Artesian water

Trapped deep below the surface of the outback is a source of water that is more than two million years old. This water is called artesian water. Artesian water is stored underground in layers of aquifers, or rock that can hold water. Below the aquifers is solid rock called bedrock. Between the aquifers are heavy layers of earth and rock that do not contain water. These layers put pressure on the aquifers. When holes, called bores, are dug into the ground to reach the aquifers, the pressure causes the water to come to the surface. Springs appear in places where the pressure is so great that artesian water explodes from cracks in the earth's surface. The Great Artesian Basin, in eastern Australia, is the country's largest source of artesian water.

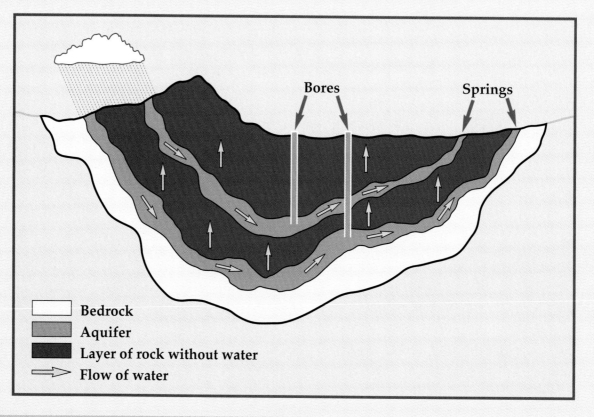

Bores   Springs

□ Bedrock
▨ Aquifer
■ Layer of rock without water
⇨ Flow of water

Islands all around

Australia's territory includes more than 150 islands. The largest island, off the south coast, is Tasmania. It was named after Abel Tasman, the Dutch navigator who landed on the island in 1642. Tasmania has almost every kind of landscape, including mountains, beaches, farmland, lush valleys, sand dunes, rivers, waterfalls, and rainforests. Unlike Australia's mainland, it does not have any large flat, deserts, such as the outback. Many of the other islands are smaller and uninhabited.

The Great Barrier Reef

The Great Barrier Reef lies off Australia's northeast coast. It is made up of nearly 3,000 individual reefs and islands that cover an area of more than 135,100 square miles (350,000 square kilometers). Tiny animals called polyps create the reef. When the polyps are alive, they release a brightly colored liquid that hardens and becomes shell-like. When they die, they leave behind their outer skeletons. As more liquid is released and as polyps attach themselves to other polyps' skeletons, the reef grows. Unfortunately, the reefs are threatened by tourists who take pieces of the reef as souvenirs; by digging done for oil exploration, and sand and coal mining; by pollution caused by fishing boats; and by crown-of-thorns starfish, which eat the coral. Many environmental groups are working to protect the reef and the plants and animals that live there.

Fraser Island, off the coast of Queensland, is the world's largest sand island.

Welcome to the outback!

The farther you move into the center of Australia, the farther you move into the outback. Australia's rural areas are called "the bush" because the land is rugged and untamed. The more remote part of Australia, made up mostly of desert, is called "the outback."

A desert land

The Great Sandy Desert, in the northwest; the Great Victoria Desert, in the southwest; and the Simpson and Gibson Deserts, in central Australia, are the four major deserts in Australia's interior. At 100,000 square miles (259,000 square kilometers), the Simpson Desert is larger than most U.S. states.

The size, weather, and wildlife of the deserts vary. The Great Sandy Desert and Great Victoria Desert are made up almost entirely of bright red sand. The Simpson Desert is dusty and pebbly, with a few plants, shrubs, and trees that can survive in extreme temperatures with little water. The Gibson Desert has grasslands, low bushes, and rugged plains. The Nullarbor Plain is a 400-mile (640-kilometer) expanse of land that is flat, dry, and completely absent of trees. In Latin, *nullus arbor* means "no tree."

Wave Rock, in Western Australia, is more than 200 million years old. It looks like a gigantic, arched wave curling in the ocean. The rock's long stripes of different colors make it look even more like water.

Uluru

Strange rock formations crop up amid the enormous sand dunes and desert plateaus of the outback. Uluru, in the Simpson Desert, is a single rock that stands 1,132 feet (345 meters) tall and is 5.8 miles (9.4 kilometers) around. That is only part of the rock! Most of Uluru, which was once known as Ayers Rock, is underground. The Aboriginals, the first known people in Australia, consider Uluru **sacred** because they believe that many **Dreamtime** events took place nearby.

Purnululu

Purnululu, or the Bungle Bungles, is a 1,160-square-mile (3,000-square-kilometer) sandstone plateau with deep gorges and rocks carved into pillar, beehive, and dome shapes by the wind. The rock pillars get their orange color from a mineral called silica and their black color from lichen, which is a fungus that attaches itself to rocks and trees.

The Devil's Marbles

Aboriginal legend has it that the Devil's Marbles were eggs laid by the Rainbow Serpent, a powerful ancestor who helped create life on Earth. The Devil's Marbles are gigantic boulders that have been eroded, or worn away, by the wind and rain. They are scattered for miles in the Northern Territory. The boulders take many shapes and sizes — some are round, some are more square, some stand alone, and others are piled on top of one another.

*These rock formations are part of Purnululu National Park, in Western Australia. **Purnululu** means "sandstone" in the local Aboriginal language.*

Scientists think that Uluru was formed over many years as sand was packed together to form the massive rock. Uluru changes color depending on the time of day, from a vibrant yellow when the sun rises to a brilliant red when the sun sets.

Imagine cool weather in June and hot weather in December. That is what it is like in the south of Australia. Winter there lasts from June to August and summer lasts from December to February. These seasons are opposite to those in North America and other areas in the western hemisphere.

Snow falls in the mountains of Tasmania and in the Australian Alps, in Victoria and New South Wales.

Different climates

The south of Australia is cooler than the north because it is closer to Antarctica, the coldest place on earth. In the north, instead of a winter and summer, there is a wet season between November and April, and a dry season between May and October. On the east and west coasts, the temperatures are mild all year long. Warm air currents and winds blowing in from the oceans keep the temperatures moderate. The center of Australia is the hottest and driest part of the country, although some areas get very cold at night. Winds whip sand and soil through the air, causing dust storms. A willy-willy is a 100-foot (30-meter) column of dust that looks like a tornado, but does not cause any damage.

Many Australians spend time in the sun, so cancer organizations run the "Slip, Slop, Slap" campaign. This campaign encourages people to slip into long-sleeved shirts and pants, slop on sunscreen, and slap on a hat before they go outside. What could this lifeguard do to protect himself even more from the sun?

Many of the bushfires near Sydney in 2001 and 2002 were started by arsonists, or people who purposely start fires.

Exploding trees

Australia's hot and dry weather leads to bushfires. Dead grass, trees, and shrubs catch fire because of the hot sun and high temperatures. The fires spread quickly, burning up large areas of land and forests. In eucalyptus forests, trees appear to explode when the oil they release catches fire.

Safety first

To protect themselves from bushfires, families trim the dry grasses and plants around their homes. Fire-risk signs along highways in the outback have different colors to indicate the amount of danger, from low to extreme. Fire warnings are sent out to people in high-risk areas. Anyone who lights a fire outside, or is not careful with objects that may cause fires, can be fined or jailed.

Monsoons and cyclones

In northwestern Australia, in an area known as "the Top End," **monsoon** rains pour down during the wet season. A monsoon rainstorm can last for days, with up to 30 inches (76 centimeters) of rain falling in 24 hours. Cyclones, which are severe storms that blow rain and high winds in from the ocean, often occur at the beginning or end of the monsoon season.

In 1974, Cyclone Tracy hit the city of Darwin, destroying 12,000 buildings and killing 66 people. Since then, new homes in Darwin have been built with special steel frames so that they will not be destroyed by storms.

The Australians

For such a large country, Australia has one of the smallest populations in the world. Australia's first peoples were the Aboriginals, who arrived on the continent at least 60,000 years ago. It is believed that they came from Asia, crossing the water by raft. Some scientists believe this was the first sea voyage taken by humans.

Over time, as many as 400 Aboriginal groups developed. Some groups were nomadic, which means they traveled from place to place in search of food and water. Others lived in settlements where they grew some crops, such as **tubers**, and caught fish using traps or fences called weirs. Nearly 10,000 years ago, the Aboriginals were joined by a group of people now known as the Torres Strait Islanders. The Torres Strait Islanders came from New Guinea, an island in the Pacific Ocean, and settled on the Torres Strait Islands, off Australia's northeastern tip.

Today's Aboriginals and Torres Strait Islanders

In 1788, British settlers arrived in Australia and gradually took over much of the land that belonged to Aboriginals and Torres Strait Islanders. Many Aboriginals and Torres Strait Islanders were killed fighting for their land, which they consider sacred, or by diseases brought by the British. Some groups, such as the Tasmanian Aboriginals, were almost entirely wiped out. Today, Aboriginals and Torres Strait Islanders make up only 1.5 percent of Australia's population. Some of their land has been returned to them, and they keep their culture alive through their art, music, dance, and storytelling.

The British

Of the 1,500 British settlers who arrived in Australia in 1788, half were convicts sent to serve time in **penal colonies**. The other half were soldiers, prison guards, and their families. In the penal colonies, the convicts, some of whom had committed crimes as minor as stealing a loaf of bread, were forced to do hard labor, building the new colony.

In 1827, Britain claimed complete ownership of Australia. With the discovery of gold and the promise of land, more English, Irish, and Scottish settlers arrived on Australia's shores. They brought to Australia new foods, stories, art, and ways of farming and manufacturing products, such as textiles. Many of Britain's traditions are still followed by the **descendants** of these **immigrants**. For example, people eat fish and chips; bangers and mash, which are sausages and mashed potatoes; and a mid-afternoon snack, called tea, as they do in England.

On Bathurst Island, off the north coast, children with painted faces await a feast. Feasts are special celebrations during which people wear traditional costumes and makeup, dance, sing, and share a meal.

Australia has not been a British colony since 1901, but it is part of the Commonwealth of Nations, a group of countries whose king or queen is the same as that of England. Many Australians are very proud of their country's ties to England.

A mix of many peoples

Australia's population is multicultural, which means that it is made up of people from all over the world. Large numbers of immigrants from Asian countries, such as China, came to Australia in the 1800s, after gold was discovered, to seek out their fortunes. The next large group of Asian immigrants came in the 1970s, after a "White Australia" policy, which did not allow people from non-European countries to move to Australia, was revoked. The policy had been put in place in 1901 to prevent competition in the goldfields. In the 1970s, people from countries in the Middle East, such as Iran, also began to immigrate to Australia.

Some Australians are descendants of immigrants who came from countries such as Greece, Italy, Yugoslavia, Hungary, Germany, Czechoslovakia, and Turkey after **World War II**. Melbourne's Greek community is the largest Greek community in the world outside Greece itself. In fact, only two cities in Greece have larger populations of Greek people than Melbourne.

A woman from Sydney, on the southeast coast, works at a tourism office where she plans tours for visitors from countries all over the world.

Many people in Australia celebrate their heritage with festivals and celebrations. At the Barossa Valley Festival, held in South Australia, German-Australians gather to enjoy German music, dancing, and food.

Coastal cities

Traveling through the outback, you might pass only one car every few hours, and you may have to drive an entire day before seeing a town. Few people make their home in this dry, barren part of the country. Instead, the majority of Australians live in cities on the coasts, where the weather is mild and the land is fertile. Most of these cities were built as penal colonies by the British on the sites of early Aboriginal settlements.

Built on low hills around a harbor, Sydney is Australia's main port city. The Harbor Bridge, which is 3,770 feet (1,149 meters) long, spans one of its bays, Lavender Bay. Some people in Sydney cross the bay by boat to get to work every day.

The oldest British settlement

Aboriginal peoples lived on the southeast coast, on the land where Sydney now stands, tens of thousands of years ago. Evidence of their settlement can be seen in the more than 2,000 sites where they carved pictures into rocks.

The city of Sydney was founded in 1788 when the first boat of convicts, soldiers, guards, and their families arrived from Britain. Today, Sydney is the largest city in Australia and the capital of New South Wales. It is filled with office buildings, sports complexes, restaurants, and hotels, and is known for its parks and beaches. Bondi Beach is one of Australia's most famous beaches. More than 2.5 million people swim, surf, and visit the nearby cafés and shops each year.

Brisbane

The Brisbane River divides Brisbane, the capital of Queensland, in two. Within the city are many interesting buildings, including the City Hall, which has a 301-foot (92-meter) tower that looms over the main square. Brisbane's oldest building is a windmill built by convicts in 1828. The windmill never provided a lot of wind power — the sails were put on backward — but it was used to grind corn. Power for the mill came from convicts running on a treadmill.

Brisbane and the river that divides it were named after Sir Thomas Brisbane, who was the British governor of Australia when the city was settled in the 1820s.

Marvelous Melbourne

Melbourne is on Australia's south coast. It was settled in the mid-1800s during the gold rush, and quickly became the most prosperous city in the country. Today, Melbourne is the capital of Victoria, and is a center for culture, food, and fashion. It has many exciting neighborhoods where people from different ethnic groups live. Chinatown is a busy district in downtown Melbourne where Chinese immigrants settled during the gold rush. The area is now mainly a shopping district where visitors sample Chinese foods, hear Chinese music, and shop for herbal medicines that have been used in China for thousands of years.

(top) Modern skyscrapers and restored buildings stand among Melbourne's gardens and parks. Melbourne is nicknamed "the Garden City" because of its 1,235 acres (500 hectares) of parks.

(right) Adelaide, the capital of South Australia, is often called "the City of Churches." Spires can be seen all around, poking up between buildings designed in French, German, Greek, and Spanish styles of architecture.

The city of churches

Adelaide was founded in 1836 as a "model colony." It was the first colony not settled by convicts. Settlers in Adelaide learned from the mistakes made by settlers in other parts of the country. For example, they grew crops that were less likely to fail in the poor soil, such as wheat, or they raised **livestock**. During the 1870s and 1880s, the success of wheat crops brought people and money to Adelaide. Many of Adelaide's buildings were constructed during this time.

Isolated Perth

Perth, the capital of Western Australia, is one of the most isolated cities in the world. It is 1,677 miles (2,700 kilometers) from the closest Australian city, Adelaide. Perth is the business and shipping center for the country's mining industry. Its business district is filled with modern office towers and colonial buildings built during the 1800s.

Capital of the nation

One of Australia's smallest cities, Canberra, is the country's capital. The name Canberra probably comes from the Aboriginal word *kamberra*, which means "meeting place." When Australia declared its independence from Britain in 1901, it had to choose a capital city. The country could not decide between Sydney and Melbourne, so an entirely new city was built. Land was taken from New South Wales, and Canberra became part of the Australian Capital Territory, just as Washington is part of the District of Columbia. To get a good look at the entire city and the surrounding countryside, people climb the Telstra Tower. This 640-foot (195-meter) **telecommunications** tower is in the middle of a **nature reserve**.

(left) People shop in London Court, a busy market in downtown Perth.

(below) Lake Burley Griffin is an artificial lake in the center of Canberra. The lake was named after the American architect Walter Burley Griffin, who designed the city.

Crops, livestock, and fishing

Only six percent of Australia's land can be used to grow crops, but the country has a strong agricultural industry. Many of the crops and animals raised in Australia were brought from other countries. Grapes, for example, were brought from Germany, and sheep and cattle were brought from England and Scotland.

Growing crops

Along the east and southeast coasts of mainland Australia and in Tasmania, grains, such as rye, barley, and millet; fruits and vegetables, such as corn, potatoes, tomatoes, carrots, apples, lemons, and bananas; and sugarcane grow. The main inland crop is wheat. Australians have developed a special type of wheat that grows well in the dry climate.

Australian wine

In the 1800s, a group of German immigrants settled in the Barossa Valley, in southern Australia. They brought a method of winemaking with them which has helped Australia become one of the world's largest wine producers. Each year, more than 800,000 tons (725,760 tonnes) of grapes are made into wine in Australia's 900 wineries.

(above) Different kinds of grapes make different kinds of wine. Red grapes make red wines, and green grapes make white wines. In the Barossa Valley, many vineyards grow red grapes.

(left) A farmer inspects a harvest of peaches lying in the sun on his farm in Murray Riverland, in South Australia.

Men who train to work on cattle or sheep stations are sometimes called "jackaroos." Women are called "jillaroos."

Cattle and sheep stations

There are ten times more sheep than people in Australia. Sheep and cattle are raised on huge ranches, called stations, in northern and central Australia. The Anna Creek Station, in the Simpson Desert, is the largest cattle station in the world. It covers more than 11,580 square miles (30,110 square kilometers), which makes it five times larger than the largest cattle ranch in the United States. The stations are big because there is very little vegetation and water in the region, so the animals need a larger area in which to graze, or feed.

Australia's sheep farmers produce lamb, **mutton**, and wool. Australia is the world's top producer of wool. Merino wool is one of the most common types. A large Merino sheep yields as much as 18 pounds (8 kilograms) of wool. The wool is removed by shearers, who use electric cutters. Very skilled shearers can remove all the wool from a sheep in one long piece.

A fisher from Kalbarri, in Western Australia, displays a rock lobster that he caught in one of his traps. Eight species of rock lobster live in the Pacific, Southern, and Indian Oceans, off Australia's coasts.

From the oceans and rivers

The waters surrounding Australia are filled with more than 1,500 edible species of seafood, including prawns, clams, mussels, and scallops. Fish, such as salmon and flounder, are also found in rivers and lakes inland. Australians eat much of their country's fish, often barbecuing it, and **export** the rest to countries such as Japan.

Changing industries

Australia's industries have grown rapidly in recent years. The main industries are food processing and manufacturing cars, electronics, textiles, clothing, steel, and chemicals. These goods are exported to many countries, such as England, Japan, the United States, Taiwan, Hong Kong, and Indonesia. Recently, service industries, such as banking, sales, construction, and especially tourism, have become increasingly important to Australia's economy.

Searching for gold

Australia has one of the richest mining industries in the world. Iron is mined in Western Australia; bauxite, copper, silver, and coal are mined in Queensland; zinc, lead, and coal are mined in New South Wales; and gold is mined throughout the country. In 1851, Edward Hargraves, a **prospector** from England, discovered gold near Bathurst, in southeast Australia. Within a month, 1,000 people had come to Australia from countries such as China, the United States, and England, leaving behind their jobs and homes to search for gold. Soon, people began to find gold all over the country. Within ten years, Australia's population doubled because of all the goldseekers arriving on its shores.

(left) Many tourists come to Australia each year to dive on the Great Barrier Reef.

(top) Chemicals produced in this factory in Melbourne are sold to countries such as the United States for use in cleaning products.

22

Mining methods

A hundred and fifty years ago, people crawled into dangerous mining shafts and used picks to chip away at rocks in search of gold. Today, miners use dynamite and machines to extract the metal from the ground. They can even collect smaller traces of gold, called tailings. Tailings are left over after the ore, or gold, has been removed from the rock.

Dirt that is rich in gold tailings is removed from the Tanami gold mine, in the Northern Territory.

"Fire of the desert"

According to an Aboriginal legend, opals, which are minerals used as gemstones, were made by a rainbow that fell to earth. Opals are sometimes called "the fire of the desert" because of their flashing, changing colors. When you move an opal, colors such as blue, pink, green, and yellow can be seen.

When opals are mined, they are rough and unpolished. Cutters remove the stone around the opal, then shape and polish it so all its colors can be seen.

The British discovered opals in Australia in 1911. Today, more than 90 percent of the opals sold throughout the world are mined in Queensland, South Australia, and New South Wales. Coober Pedy is a major opal mining town in South Australia. The temperatures in Coober Pedy are so hot during the day and so cold at night that miners and their families live in houses that are completely underground. The temperature underground is always a comfortable 77° Fahrenheit (25° Celsius).

Nuclear power

Uranium is a silvery-white metal that is mined mostly in the Northern Territory and Western Australia. It is used to create energy in nuclear power stations in countries such as Japan and China. Nuclear power is important because the earth's supply of coal, oil, and natural gas, which are also used to create energy, are disappearing. Nuclear power can also be dangerous. It can be used in nuclear warfare, and the waste created while generating nuclear energy is harmful to animals and humans. Some Australians think that their country should not mine or export uranium because of these dangers.

What grows in Australia?

Australia is home to thousands of species of plants, birds, mammals, and insects that are not found anywhere else in the world. Of the 800 species of wattles, more than 600 grow only in Australia. Wattles, which are also called acacias, range from low bushes with small flowers to large trees, such as the babul and blackwood.

(above) Cycads and grass trees are living fossils. They are considered living fossils because they have existed since the Jurassic era, which began 195 million years ago. Unlike other plants, they have not adapted or changed in all that time.

(below) The golden wattle, Australia's national flower, has long spikes and golden blooms in the spring.

Unusual flowers

Australia's wildflowers include Christmas bells, orchids, Sturt's desert peas, and kangaroo paws. Sturt's desert peas, which are South Australia's flower, are sometimes called "the flowers of blood." The flowers have red petals and gray-green leaves. Kangaroo paws have long stems covered in fine hairs. They can be red or green, with small flowers during the spring and summer.

The wood from eucalyptus trees is used for timber, and the oil from their leaves is used to make cough drops and other medicines.

Eucalyptus trees

The eucalyptus is the most common tree in Australia. There are more than 500 species, some that grow as tall as 25-story buildings. Eucalyptus trees in drier areas have smaller leaves than those in areas with a lot of rainfall. The leaves have a layer of wax on top that prevents water from evaporating, and some eucalyptus trees turn their leaves away from the sun when it is very hot. Eucalyptus trees are also known as gum trees because small, sticky beads of sap form on their trunks.

Boabs, also called baobabs, are trees that are shaped like bottles. Their wide trunks hold water. Farmers in the outback once tapped holes in the trees and used the water stored inside to feed their livestock.

Huon pines

The Huon pine, which is found along the Huon River in Tasmania, grows very slowly and lives for a very long time. Some Huon pines are believed to be more than 2,200 years old. In the 1800s, the British began using the Huon pine's strong wood to build ships. Even though the tree is now **endangered**, the demand for its wood is still high. Many environmental groups are fighting to ensure that the Huon pine does not become **extinct**.

The scarlet banksia grows on shrubs that are up to twelve feet (three meters) tall.

Many kinds of marsupials hop, run, and climb throughout Australia. A marsupial is a type of mammal that gives birth to its young before the young is fully developed. The undeveloped baby climbs into a pouch on its mother and continues to grow there until it is fully formed. The word "marsupial" comes from the Latin word *marsupium*, meaning "pouch." Kangaroos, koalas, and wallabies, which are like small kangaroos, are marsupials. Wombats and bandicoots are marsupials that both look like large rodents.

Tasmanian devils are a type of marsupial that some people believe are dangerous. In fact, most Tasmanian devils are harmless. They are scavengers, which means that they eat prey left behind by other predators.

Climbing koalas

Koalas have long, strong forearms and paws with two thumbs and long claws that allow them to hold on tightly to branches as they climb trees. Koalas are most often seen dozing in eucalyptus trees. When they are not sleeping, they are eating eucalyptus leaves, which is their main source of food. The oil in the leaves keeps the koalas **hydrated** so they can go for long periods of time without drinking water. Koalas also eat gravel and soil. The gravel helps them digest the leaves, and the soil provides them with **minerals**, such as sodium, which the leaves do not have.

Jumping kangaroos

One of Australia's national symbols is the kangaroo. A kangaroo's long back legs and tail are so strong that it can jump the length of a school bus. Of the 45 types of kangaroos in Australia, the most common are the gray and red kangaroos. Red kangaroos are nicknamed "big reds" because males grow to be more than 6 feet (1.8 meters) tall — taller than the average human being. Their feet are so big that if they wore shoes, they would need a size 22. Female kangaroos grow to be 4.5 feet (1.4 meters) tall. The smallest kangaroo is the musky rat-kangaroo. This strange-looking animal is the size of a rat, has the body and tail of a rat, but has long feet like a kangaroo.

The word "koala" comes from the word **coolah** *or* **koolah**, *which means "no drink" in Dharug, an Aboriginal language spoken in the Sydney region.*

Unusual monotremes

A monotreme is a mammal that lays eggs instead of giving birth to a live baby. Usually, only birds and reptiles lay eggs. The only two types of monotremes in the world, the echidna and the platypus, live in Australia. The echidna is a small animal that looks like a porcupine. It has long claws, quills, and a tube-like bill with a hole in it through which it sucks ants, the main part of its diet. The platypus looks as if it is made up of parts from many animals. It has webbed feet and a bill, like a duck; its body is covered in thick, waterproof fur, like an otter; and it has a tail, like a beaver. The male platypus also has spurs on the backs of its hind legs which are connected to a poisonous sack. To protect itself and the female's eggs, the platypus drives its spurs into the animal or human that is threatening it.

For protection, the echidna digs itself into a hole so that the only thing a predator can grasp is its quills.

The platypus lives in Australia's rivers and creeks, where it feeds mostly on shrimp, worms, and tadpoles.

The frill-necked lizard has a large flap of skin around its head that it spreads out when threatened by predators.

Busy termites

Small insects called termites build enormous wedge-shaped **magnetic** mounds in many parts of the outback. The mounds, which termites make by sticking together chewed up wood or feces, face north to south to line up with the earth's magnetic poles.

Magnetic mounds have complicated passageways, chambers, and air holes.

(right) Cassowaries are large, flightless birds that crash through the undergrowth of the northern rainforests using a bony growth on their head, called a casque. When threatened, cassowaries jump up, both feet at once, and strike predators with the razor-sharp claws on their feet.

Keep out!

Thousands of miles of fences have been built in Australia to keep animals such as rabbits and dingoes from certain areas. Millions of rabbits kill the grass and plant life that farmers need to feed their sheep and cattle. Dingoes, a type of wild dog, are sometimes kept as pets, but most live in the wilderness where they prey on livestock. The Dingo Fence, which runs from Queensland, through New South Wales, to South Australia, keeps dingoes away from livestock. At 3,300 miles (5,309 kilometers), it is the longest fence in the world.

Birds of a feather

More than 740 species of birds make their home in Australia. Kookaburras live in the holes of eucalyptus trees in Australia's woodlands and grasslands. They are known for their call, which sounds like laughter. Lyre birds, which live in the rainforests, imitate many sounds, including other animals and even car horns. Emus, the second largest birds in the world, cannot fly. They live in Australia's woods, scrublands, and grasslands. Unlike most birds, male emus build the nests, keep the eggs warm, and raise the young. One emu egg weighs 20 ounces (567 grams), which is about the same weight as ten hen's eggs.

Danger in the wild

The list of dangerous animals in Australia is very long. Large, flat fish called numbrays shoot up to 200 volts of electricity through their prey to kill them. Some shells, including certain species of cone shells, release venom, or poison, through their teeth or through a long feeding tube. The venom can harm people who pick up the shells.

The ten most poisonous snakes in the world are all found in Australia. The deadliest snakes are the taipan and tiger snake. The taipan's venom is 50 times more deadly than a cobra's.

"Salties"

Two types of crocodiles live in Australia. One is the freshwater crocodile and the other is the saltwater crocodile, which Australians call "salties." Saltwater crocodiles live mainly around the north coast of Australia. These reptiles kill their prey by grabbing it with their strong jaws, pulling it under water, and rolling it over until it drowns.

"Salties" can grow to be as big as a car.

The venomous funnel-web spider lives in parts of New South Wales, Victoria, South Australia, and Tasmania.

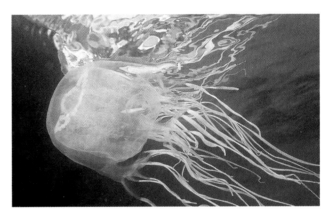

Box jellyfish, which are also called sea wasps, marine stingers, or stingers, have 60 tentacles that are each 15 feet (4.6 meters) long. Some swimmers wear pantyhose on their arms and legs to protect themselves from the deadly stings of the jellyfish's tentacles.

The great white shark

Many types of sharks, including the great white shark, live off Australia's coasts. The average great white shark is between 12 and 16 feet (3.7 and 4.9 meters) long, but some grow to be 19 to 21 feet (5.8 to 6.4 meters) long. The great white shark's 3,000 teeth, which are as sharp as knives, are strong enough to saw through wood. Sharks sometimes attack humans in the waters off Australia, but scientists believe that sharks do not like the taste of human flesh. The sharks mistake humans for seals, sea lions, and other prey.

Life on the Great Barrier Reef

Many species of gorgonian coral grow on the Great Barrier Reef. One type is the gorgonian fan, which has fan-shaped branches.

Swimming among the coral

There is a lot of activity among the coral of the Great Barrier Reef. Stingrays, which are large, flat fish with poisonous barbs, or spikes, in their tails hide in the shallow waters of the reef. Sea cucumbers climb over the coral with their many rows of feet. Their long tentacles help them catch sea animals to eat. Sea snails have hard shells that protect them from predators. They feed on **algae** that grow on the coral.

If you look deeper in the water, you will find other fascinating animals crawling on the reef, such as starfish, sea urchins, spiny lobsters, and mantis shrimp. Mantis shrimp have pincers they can shoot forward so fast they can smash a crab's shell. There are also beautifully colored fish, such as the parrot fish, wrasse, and angelfish. Many of these fish swim carefully through the reef, avoiding predators and other dangerous organisms, such as anemones. Anemones use their long tentacles to sting their prey.

The Great Barrier Reef is home to at least 4,000 types of **mollusks**, 1,500 species of fish, and 400 species of coral. Two main types of coral give the reef its brilliant colors — hard coral and soft coral. Hard coral, such as brain coral, looks like gnarled rocks. Soft coral, such as gorgonial coral, looks like branches swaying in the ocean's current. With its many **tentacles**, soft coral catches and eats **zooplankton** floating in the water.

Fish swim through a garden of hard and soft coral.

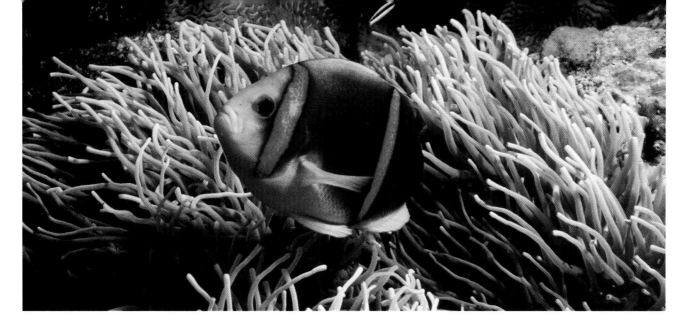

The clown fish covers itself in a protective slime so that it can swim among the anemone's tentacles, feeding on leftovers from the anemone's meal.

Beyond the reef

Sharks, humpback whales, and dolphins swim in the cold, deep waters beyond the reef. The humpback whale, which is a mammal, breathes through a blow hole on the top of its head. A male humpback whale can grow to be 42 feet (12.8 meters) long and weigh 25 tons (22.7 tonnes). Female humpback whales are larger. They can grow to be 45 feet (13.7 meters) long and weigh 35 tons (31.8 tonnes).

This humpback whale breaches, or performs a back flip, in the waters of the Coral Sea, off the Great Barrier Reef.

One of the most curious things about humpback whales are the sounds they make beneath the water, called songs. Some songs last between 10 and 20 minutes. No one is sure how the whales make the sounds, but some scientists believe the sounds come from the whales' breathing.

Fire urchins, known for their extremely poisonous barbs, crawl along the Great Barrier Reef.

Glossary

Aboriginal A member of the earliest known people to live in a country

adapt To adjust or change to fit new conditions

algae An organism that lives mainly in water

clever-man An older, respected member of an Aboriginal group who is believed to have special powers

descendant A person who can trace his or her family roots to a certain family or group

Dreamtime An Aboriginal name for the time in which the world was created

endangered In danger of extinction

evaporate To change from a liquid to a gas. Clouds and mist are evaporated water.

export To sell goods to another country

extinct No longer in existence, as with dinosaurs

fertile Able to produce abundant crops and vegetation

hydrated Having enough water to remain healthy

immigrant A person who settles in another country

Latin The language of the ancient Romans

livestock Farm animals

magnetic Naturally aligned with north and south

mineral A naturally occurring, non-living substance obtained through mining

mollusk An animal with a soft body and usually a hard shell

monsoon A strong wind that changes direction depending on the season

mutton The meat of a fully grown sheep

nature reserve A park where plants and animals are protected from hunters and are observed by scientists and tourists

penal colony A place in another country where criminals are sent for punishment

prospector A person who explores an area for minerals or precious metals

rainforest A forest in a tropical area that receives a lot of rain

sacred Having special religious significance

southern hemisphere The southern half of Earth, below the equator

stagnant Not moving or flowing

telecommunication The science and technology of sending electronic messages, for example, by telephone, computer, radio, or television

tentacle A long flexible feeler used for moving, touching, or grabbing

tuber A fleshy edible root

World War II A war fought by countries around the world from 1939 to 1945

zooplankton Tiny animal organisms that float in fresh or salt water and provide food for larger organisms

Index

Aboriginals 6, 7, 10, 11, 14, 16, 23
Adelaide 18
artesian water 8
billabongs 8
birds 4, 28
Brisbane 5, 6, 17
British 14–15, 16, 17, 19, 23, 25
bushfires 13
Canberra 5, 19
climate 10, 12–13, 16, 20, 23
coasts 4, 5, 6, 12, 16
continental drift 4
coral 9, 30
crocodiles 4, 8, 29
crops 14, 18, 20
cyclones 13

Darling River 8
deserts 10
Devil's Marbles 11
dingoes 28
echidnas 27
eucalyptus 6, 8, 13, 25, 26
farming 14, 18, 20
fish 14, 21, 29, 30–31
flowers 24, 25
forests 6, 8, 9, 13, 28
gold 14, 15, 18, 22–23
Great Barrier Reef 4, 9, 30–31
immigrants 14, 15, 18, 20
islands 4, 9, 14
kangaroos 4, 26
koalas 4, 26
Lake Eyre 7
marsupials 26

Melbourne 18, 19
mining 14, 15, 18, 22–23
monsoons 13
mountains 6, 8, 9, 12
Mount Kosciuzko 6
Murray River 8
nuclear power 23
opals 23
outback 4, 5, 8, 10–11, 13, 16, 25, 28
penal colonies 14, 16, 17
Perth 19
platypuses 27
playas 7
Purnululu 11
rabbits 28
sandstorms 12
sharks 29, 31
sheep stations 21

snakes 29
Sydney 13, 16, 19
Tasmania 4, 9, 12, 14, 25, 26
termites 28
Three Sisters 6–7
Torres Strait Islanders 14
trees 6, 8, 9, 13, 24, 25, 26
Twelve Apostles 6
Uluru 10–11
Wave Rock 10
whales 31
wildlife 4, 8–9, 24–31
winemaking 20